CAMBRIDGE PRIMARY
Science

Learner's Book

Jon Board and Alan Cross

CAMBRIDGE
UNIVERSITY PRESS

University Printing House, Cambridge CB2 8BS, United Kingdom

One Liberty Plaza, 20th Floor, New York, NY 10006, USA

477 Williamstown Road, Port Melbourne, VIC 3207, Australia

314–321, 3rd Floor, Plot 3, Splendor Forum, Jasola District Centre,
New Delhi – 110025, India

79 Anson Road, #06–04/06, Singapore 079906

José Abascal, 56–1°, 28003 Madrid, Spain

Cambridge University Press is part of the University of Cambridge.

It furthers the University's mission by disseminating knowledge in the pursuit of
education, learning and research at the highest international levels of excellence.

www.cambridge.org
Information on this title: www.cambridge.org/9781107611382

© Cambridge University Press 2014

This publication is in copyright. Subject to statutory exception
and to the provisions of relevant collective licensing agreements,
no reproduction of any part may take place without the written
permission of Cambridge University Press.

First published 2014

40 39 38 37 36 35 34 33 32 31 30 29 28
Printed in Great Britain by Ashford Colour Press Ltd.

A catalogue record for this publication is available from the British Library

ISBN 978-1-107-61138-2 Paperback

Cambridge University Press has no responsibility for the persistence or accuracy
of URLs for external or third-party internet websites referred to in this publication,
and does not guarantee that any content on such websites is, or will remain,
accurate or appropriate. Information regarding prices, travel timetables, and other
factual information given in this work is correct at the time of first printing but
Cambridge University Press does not guarantee the accuracy of such information
thereafter.

Cover artwork: Bill Bolton

....

NOTICE TO TEACHERS
References to Activities contained in these resources are provided 'as is' and information
provided is on the understanding that teachers and technicians shall undertake a thorough
and appropriate risk assessment before undertaking any of the Activities listed. Cambridge
University Press makes no warranties, representations or claims of any kind concerning the
Activities. To the extent permitted by law, Cambridge University Press will not be liable for
any loss, injury, claim, liability or damage of any kind resulting from the use of
the Activities.

Introduction

The *Cambridge Primary Science* series has been developed to match the Cambridge International Examinations Primary Science curriculum framework. It is a fun, flexible and easy to use course that gives both learners and teachers the support they need. In keeping with the aims of the curriculum itself, it encourages learners to actively engage with the content, and develop enquiry skills as well as subject knowledge.

This Learner's Book for Stage 1 covers all the content from Stage 1 of the curriculum framework. The topics are covered in the order in which they are presented in the curriculum, with only one or two exceptions, for easy navigation. But they can be taught in any order that is appropriate to you.

The content pages contain many images and questions that you can use as a basis for class discussions. The emphasis in this stage is on linking what learners know about everyday life to scientific ideas.

Throughout the book, you will find ideas for practical activities which will help learners to develop their Scientific Enquiry skills as well as introduce them to the thrill of scientific discovery.

Check your progress questions at the end of each unit can be used to assess learners' understanding.

We strongly advise you to use the Teacher's Resource for Stage 1 ISBN 978-1-107-61146-7, alongside this book. This resource contains extensive guidance on all the topics, ideas for classroom activities, and guidance notes on all the activities presented in this Learner's Book. You will also find a large collection of worksheets, and answers to all the questions from the Stage 1 products.

Also available is the Activity Book for Stage 1, ISBN 978-1-107-61142-9. This book offers a variety of exercises to help learners consolidate understanding, practise vocabulary, apply knowledge to new situations and develop enquiry skills. Learners can complete the exercises in class or be given them as homework.

We hope you enjoy using this series.

With best wishes,
the Cambridge Primary Science team.

Contents

1 Being alive

1.1	Animals and plants alive!	6
1.2	Local environments	8
1.3	Animal babies	10
1.4	Healthy food and drink	12
1.5	Check your progress	14

2 Growing plants

2.1	Plant parts	16
2.2	Growing seeds	18
2.3	Plants and light	20
2.4	Check your progress	22

3 Ourselves

3.1	We are similar	24
3.2	We are different	26
3.3	Our bodies	28
3.4	Our fantastic senses	30
3.5	Check your progress	32

4 Materials in my world

4.1	What is it made of?	34
4.2	Using materials	36
4.3	Sorting materials	38
4.4	Check your progress	40

5 Pushes and pulls

5.1	In the playground	42
5.2	How toys work	44
5.3	Pushes and pulls around us	46
5.4	Changing movement	48
5.5	Check your progress	50

6 Hearing sounds

6.1	Where do sounds come from?	52
6.2	Our ears	54
6.3	Sounds move	56
6.4	Check your progress	58

Reference	60
Glossary and index	62
Acknowledgements	69

1 Being alive

1.1 Animals and plants alive!

Words to learn
living   plant
animal   alive
non-living look

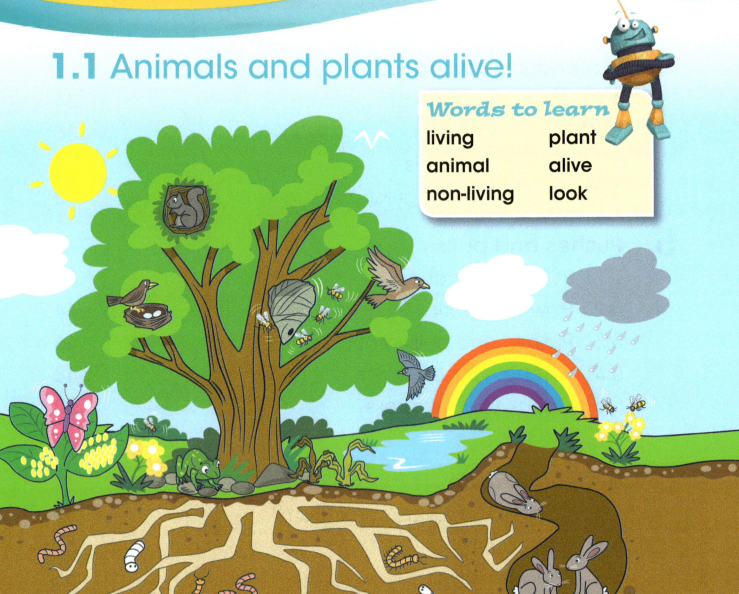

Can you see a living plant?

Can you see a living animal?
Can you see things that have never been alive?

The Sun is hot but it is not alive. It is a non-living thing.

Activity 1.1

You will need:
a clipboard • a digital camera

What living things can we find?

Go outside to look at living things.

Photograph or draw those you find.

Look for the largest living thing you can see.

Look for the smallest living thing you can find.

Try to find six living things.

Talk about the photos below with your friends.

Which photos show things that are alive?

Which photos show things that are non-living?

How do you know which things are alive?

What you have learnt

- Some things are alive.
- Some things have never been alive.

1 Being alive

1.2 Local environments

Each living thing needs a place to live and lives in a local environment.

Words to learn
environment farm
pet compare

Look at each animal. Look at each plant. Where does it live? Why does it live there?

Animals can be found in natural environments.

They can also be found on a farm, in a zoo and in homes as a pet.

Activity 1.2a

Where do plants grow?

You will need:
a clipboard • a digital camera

Think about where you will find plants growing outside.

Go outside and look at the plants. Where do they grow?

Why do they grow where they do?

Compare how many plants you find in different environments.

Activity 1.2b

Birds come to school

Have you seen birds at school? Where do you see them?

Can we make the environment better for them?

How could we make a feeding table?

Make a drawing to show how you could help the birds.

What you have learnt

- Each living thing lives in a local environment.
- The local environment gives them a home, food and water.

1 Being alive

All animals make babies. The babies grow up into adults.

A human mother usually has just one baby at a time. Why?

Some animals have lots of babies.

Birds and rabbits can have eight or nine young at a time.

Activity 1.3

Make a nursery for a baby animal

Make a model nursery for a baby animal.

You will need:
modelling material or a construction kit • cardboard • scissors • glue • sticky tape

Make sure you include food, water and a home.

What you have learnt

- Humans and other animals have babies.
- Young animals grow into adults.

1 Being alive

1.4 Healthy food and drink

Do you want to grow up healthy and strong?

Eat lots of healthy food like fruit and vegetables. Also drink lots of water.

Words to learn
healthy   food
fat   sugar
salt

Which lunch bag is healthier?

Activity 1.4

My healthy plate

Draw your own plate of food for today.

Draw, or stick on, pictures of these foods.

Compare your plate with a plate of healthy food.

You will need:
pictures of food

Fruit and vegetables come from plants. They are full of good things for your body.

They do not have too much fat, sugar and salt. Too much of these things is not healthy.

What you have learnt

- Some foods and drinks are healthy.
- Foods and drinks with too much fat, sugar and salt are not healthy.
- Drinking lots of water is healthy.

1.5 Check your progress

1. Matt, the librarian, is in a muddle. He has dropped some books.

   Which books go on each shelf?

2. Here are two local environments.

   Which animals live in each environment?

3 Can you match each adult animal with its young?

4 Which of these foods are healthy foods?

1 Being alive   15

Growing plants

2.1 Plant parts

Plants have many parts.

Words to learn
fruit   flower
stem   leaf
roots   name

Look at this garden. There are many different plants in this garden.

Can you see a leaf?

Can you see a flower?

Can you see a stem?

Can you see any roots?

Activity 2.1

Plant hunt

Go outside to look for plants.

You will need:
a magnifying glass

Can you name the parts?

What you have learnt

- Plants have roots, stems and leaves.
- Sometimes plants have flowers or fruit.

2.2 Growing seeds

This is how a seed will grow into a plant.

Words to learn
seed   grow
water

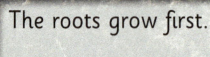

The roots grow first.

Then the stem and leaves.

Activity 2.2

Growing seeds

Ana and Marta are growing seeds.

You will need:
two clear containers
a roll of paper • seeds
a watering can

Ana gives her seeds some water. Marta forgets to water her seeds.

What do you think will happen?

Grow some seeds to find out.

Small seeds can grow into big plants.

What you have learnt

- Seeds grow into plants.
- Seeds need water to grow.

2 Growing plants 19

2.3 Plants and light

Why is this plant bent?

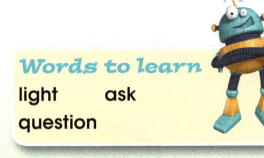

Words to learn
light   ask
question

It is growing towards the light.

2 Growing plants

Activity 2.3

Do plants need light to grow?

Ali wants to ask a question.

You will need:
two small plants • a box to cover one plant

Do plants need light to grow?

Ali covers one plant with a box. He leaves the other one in the light.

What do you think will happen?

Try this yourself to find out.

Why are these plants all facing the same way?

What you have learnt

- Plants need light to grow.

2 Growing plants 21

2.4 Check your progress

1 Can you name the parts of this plant? Use these words.

roots   leaf   flower   stem   fruit

2 What do these plants need?

3 Can you help Amy?

a How can she grow a flower?
b What does the plant need?

3 Ourselves

3.1 We are similar

Look at the children.

Words to learn
similar

The children are talking about why they are similar. That means ways in which they are like each other.

In what other ways are the children similar?

Activity 3.1a

You will need:
a mirror

How are we similar?

Look at yourself.

Work with your friends.

Look at your clothes. Look at your faces. Look at your bodies.

Talk about how you are similar to your friends.

Make drawings to show how you are similar.

Activity 3.1b

Things we like

Talk to your friends about things you like.

Draw the things that you and your friends like. Do you like similar things?

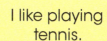

I like playing tennis.

So do I!

What you have learnt

- We are similar in lots of ways.

3 Ourselves   25

3.2 We are different

The picture shows learners at school. They are all similar.

Words to learn
different

Talk about why they are similar.

The learners are not all the same. They are all a little different.

Talk about why they are different.

3 Ourselves

Activity 3.2

Our differences

Talk to your friends about how you are all different.

Talk about hair, skin, height, clothes, glasses, games you like, things you do not like.

See if you can sort yourselves into groups.

Look at these children. They are different.

Which child has dark hair?

Which children have brown eyes?

Which children are girls?

What you have learnt

- We can see how we are similar.
- We can see how we are different.

3.3 Our bodies

Look at the main parts of the body.

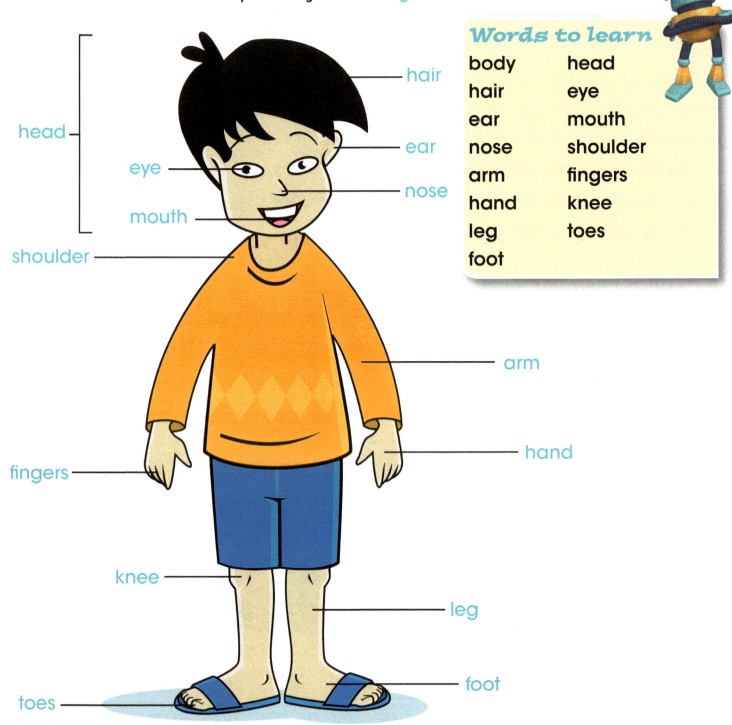

Words to learn

body	head
hair	eye
ear	mouth
nose	shoulder
arm	fingers
hand	knee
leg	toes
foot	

Which other parts of the body can you name?

Can you count your body parts?

How many legs do you have?

How many fingers do you have?

How many mouths do you have?

Activity 3.3

Parts of the body

Cut out a picture of a person. Label it with these body parts:

> head   hair   ear
> mouth   shoulder   arm
> leg   knee   foot   hand

What are the main body parts?

What are the most important body parts?

You will need:
a picture of a person
scissors

What you have learnt

- We can see and name the main parts of the body.

3 Ourselves   29

3.4 Our fantastic senses

Our senses help us know what is around us.

The girl is blindfolded. Each eye is covered. She cannot see.

Words to learn
senses   see
touch   smell
taste   hear
feel   tongue

She is playing a game to pin the tail on the horse.

She can touch, smell, taste and hear.

3 Ourselves

Activity 3.4

You will need:
a range of objects
a cloth or paper bag

Touch and feel game

Put objects in the bag.

Ask your friend to *feel* the objects.

Can they say how the objects feel?

Can they tell others about the objects?

We use our ears to hear, our eyes to see, our nose to smell, our skin to touch, and our *tongue* to taste.

Animals have senses too.

Look at these animals and say how they can do these things.

Why do they need senses? What can they find out using their senses?

What you have learnt

- Our senses tell us about the world around us.

3 Ourselves

31

3.5 Check your progress

1 How are the hands the same?

How are the hands different?

2 Ten children all have hair. They are similar.

They have different colours of hair.

Their hair colours were written in a chart.

How many children have red hair?

Which colour is most common?

Hair colour	Number of children
	✓ ✓ ✓ ✓ ✓
	✓
	✓ ✓ ✓ ✓

3 Point to these parts of the child's body.

> head   eyes   hair
> shoulders   nose   toes
> arms   hands

4 Lina has her eyes closed. She cannot see.

Can she hear?

Can she taste?

Can she smell?

Can she touch?

5 Can the cat see?

Can the bird hear?

How do the senses help the cat?

How do the senses help the bird?

3 Ourselves

4 Materials in my world

4.1 What is it made of?

There are lots of materials in the world around you.

Words to learn
materials	metal
plastic	wood
rock	fabric
rubber	paper
glass	concrete

The children are looking at materials.

Can you find metal, plastic, wood, rock, fabric and rubber?

What other materials can you see?

34 4 Materials in my world

Activity 4.1

You will need:
a clipboard • a magnifying glass

Materials we find

Walk around your classroom or school.

Look for things made from metals, paper, glass, fabrics and concrete.

Write down which materials you see.

What do they look like? What do they feel like?

Look closely at some materials. Can you see small parts of the material?

A car is made from many different materials. Metal is used for the car body. Rubber is used for the tyres. Fabric is used for the seat covers.

What you have learnt

- There are lots of different materials.
- Common materials are wood, glass, plastic, paper, metal, concrete and fabric.

4 Materials in my world   35

4.2 Using materials

What materials can you see?
Are they strong? Are they flexible?

Are they warm or soft to the touch?

Can you see through them?

Words to learn
strong   flexible
soft   properties
rough   smooth
magnifying glass
fibres

Talk about why each material has been chosen for the job.

Strong, flexible and soft are different properties of materials.

Activity 4.2

You will need: four or five different fabrics • a magnifying glass

Rough and soft fabrics

Some fabrics are soft,
some are rough,
some are smooth.

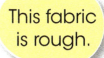
This fabric is rough.

Which fabric do you think will be the smoothest?

Look at the fabrics with a magnifying glass. Feel them.

Put them in order from the smoothest to the roughest.

Were you right?

Have your friends put the fabrics in the same order?

A fabric has many small threads called fibres. The way in which these fibres are woven together makes the fabric feel rough or smooth.

What you have learnt

- Different materials have different properties.
- Materials with different properties are used for different jobs.

4 Materials in my world

4.3 Sorting materials

You can recycle materials.

This is good for the environment.

Words to learn

recycle   group
sort   shiny
test

This plastic bottle can be recycled. It could be made into another bottle.

The fabric of the clothes can be used to make new clothes.

Which of these materials could be used again?

The paper can be recycled to make new paper.

The children put similar materials together in a group.

What groups would you make?

Activity 4.3a

Grouping materials

Use a question to put the materials into groups. For example: Is it metal?

Pick the materials up and feel them.

Now use the properties of materials to *sort* them into groups. For example: Is the material warm? Is it *shiny*?

Share your groups with the class.

You will need: a set of different materials

Activity 4.3b

Testing materials

What other properties do your materials have?

Think about a simple *test* that you could use to find out.

Is it flexible? Is it strong? Is it bouncy? Is it see-through?

Use what you find out to make new groups.

Can you think of other tests?

You will need: a set of different materials

What you have learnt

- Materials can be sorted into groups based on their properties.

4 Materials in my world

4.4 Check your progress

1 What materials are used to make these objects?

Use these words.

> plastic   wood   glass   metal

2 Here are some objects made from different materials.

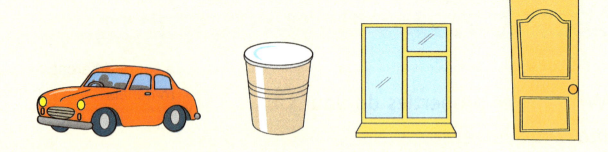

Why are these objects made from these materials?

Choose **one** of these reasons.

> glass is see-through   wood is strong
>
> plastic is light   metal is very strong

4 Materials in my world

3 Do you agree with the children?

The tyres are made of rubber because it grips well.

The tyres are made of rubber because it is slippery.

The tyres are made of rubber because rubber is black.

The tyres are made of rubber because it can't hurt you.

4 How could you sort these objects?

Is there more than one way to sort them?

Pushes and pulls

5.1 In the playground

Words to learn
moving swing
run jump
turn

How are these children moving?

5 Pushes and pulls

Activity 5.1

Moving around

Go to a playground. Find different ways to move.

I can swing.   I can run.   I can jump.   I can turn.

Tell your friends how you are moving.

Moving in space can be hard. How is the astronaut moving?

What you have learnt

- There are lots of different ways of moving.

5 Pushes and pulls

5.2 How toys work

How do these toys work?

Words to learn
push   pull

A push or a pull can make things move.

Which toys do you pull?

Which toys do you push?

5 Pushes and pulls

Activity 5.2

A moving toy

You will need:
a construction kit • an elastic band • a plastic straw or short bamboo pole • sticky tape • string

Make a push or pull toy like these.

Ahmed has made this toy.
It moves when you pull it.

Anita has made this toy.
It moves when you push it.

Talk about how you make your toy move.

What you have learnt

- Pushes and pulls can make things move.

5 Pushes and pulls   45

5.3 Pushes and pulls around us

This bulldozer is pushing.

What other machines push or pull to make things?

Activity 5.3

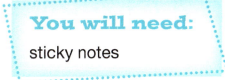

You will need:
sticky notes

Push or pull?

Look around your classroom.

Can you see things you can push or pull?

Try to push or pull them.

Were you right?

Label the things that you find.

Why do some things not move when you push them?

What you have learnt

- We have to push and pull to make things work.

5 Pushes and pulls

5.4 Changing movement

Words to learn
faster   slower
stop

Adjo is being pulled along. What is going to happen?

How can Adjo turn?

Activity 5.4

You will need:
a ball

How can balls move?

Play a game with a ball in the playground.

How can you make a ball go *faster*?

How can you make a ball go *slower*?

How can you make a ball go a different way?

How can you make a ball *stop*?

What you have learnt

- Pushes and pulls can make things go faster or slower.
- Pushes and pulls can make things go a different way.
- Pushes and pulls can make things stop.

5 Pushes and pulls   49

5.5 Check your progress

1 Is she pulling or pushing?

2 How is the boy moving?

3 How are these people moving?

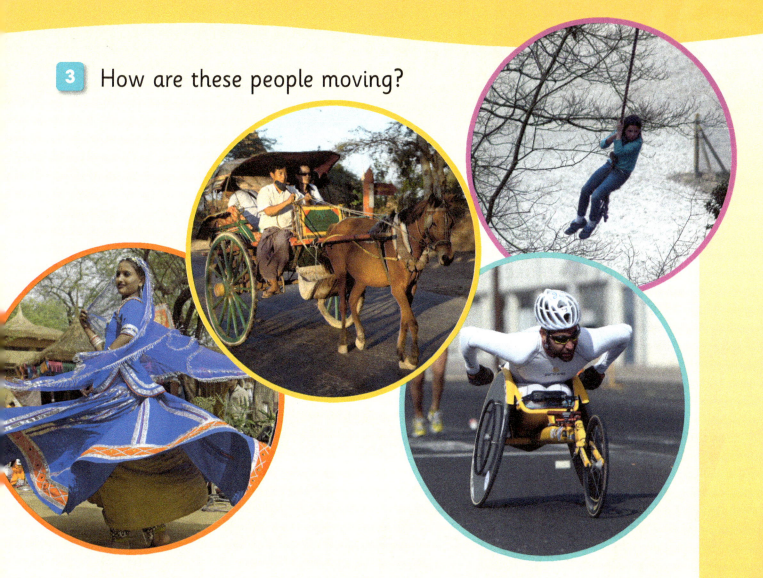

Can you find turning, swinging, pushing and pulling?

4 Vishni and Chipo are riding bicycles.

   a How can Chipo go faster?
   b How can Vishni slow down?
   c How can they turn?

5 Pushes and pulls   51

6 Hearing sounds

6.1 Where do sounds come from?

Some things make a sound.
There are lots of sounds here.

Words to learn
sound   source
voice   listen

A thing that makes a sound is called a sound source.

How many sound sources can you find?

Your voice is a sound source.

Activity 6.1

Listening to sounds

Fadi is using his ears to *listen* to sounds.
What can he hear?

What will you hear if you do this?

Try it. Close your eyes to help you listen.

Where do the sounds come from?

Try listening again. Do you hear anything different?

What you have learnt

- People, animals and other things make sounds.
- A thing that makes a sound is called a sound source.

6.2 Our ears

Hearing is one of your senses.

We hear sounds with our ears.

Words to learn
loud   quiet
soft

What are these people doing?

What do they have on their ears.

6 Hearing sounds

Activity 6.2

Loud and soft sounds

Ume is covering her ears.

Listen to a sound.

Now cover your ears with your hands. What can you hear this time?

You have stopped some of the sound going into your ears.

Doing this can stop loud sounds damaging your ears.

Tamu is listening to quiet sounds.

Listen to a sound.

Now put your hands up to your ears. Does it change what you hear?

Doing this helps you to hear soft sounds.

What you have learnt

- We hear sound when it goes into our ears.

6.3 Sounds move

Can anyone hear the man?

Why not?

Activity 6.3

You will need:
percussion instruments
a large space

How far do sounds go?

Who can hear the sound loudly?

Who can hear the sound quietly?

Try this with quiet and loud sounds.

Which can go further?

We can use a megaphone to make our voices sound louder and go further.

What you have learnt

- Sound gets quieter as it moves away from the source.

6.4 Check your progress

1 Which of these make sounds you can hear?

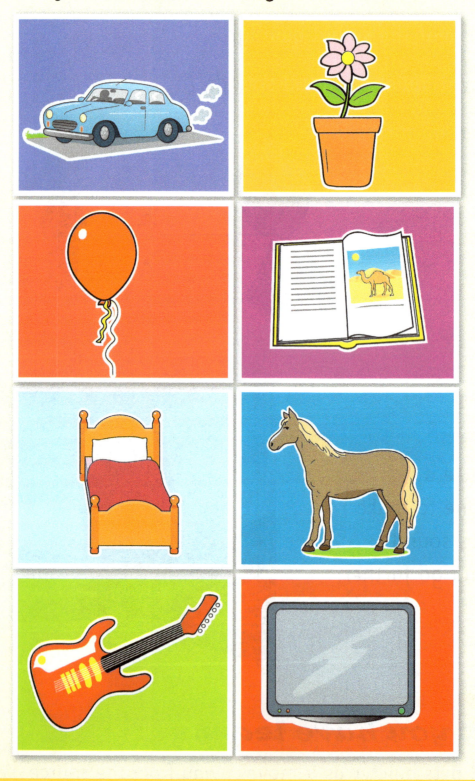

2 What might happen to this girl's ears?

3 Ben can't hear the music. What can he do?

6 Hearing sounds

Reference

This section of the Learner's Book covers some of the new scientific enquiry skills for this stage. You should refer to these skills whenever you need them.

How to find things out in science

Think of a question

Amina and Nila have planted different seeds.

Which plant will grow the fastest?

Think about what will happen

Nila says what she thinks will happen.

I think they will all grow fast.

Talk about what to do

Amina and Nila decide to look at how tall the plants are every day.

Find out

They use bricks to find out how tall the plants have grown.

Show what you find out

On the last day Amina and Nila compare the three brick towers. They tell the class what they have found out.

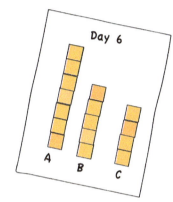

Talk about what you find out

Amina and Nila have found out that plant A grew the fastest. They have also found out that some plants grow faster than others.

Glossary and index

		Page
alive	something that is living	6
animal	a living thing that can move around and eats other living things	6
ask	use a question to find out	21
baby	the young of an animal	10
body	the whole part of a person or animal	28

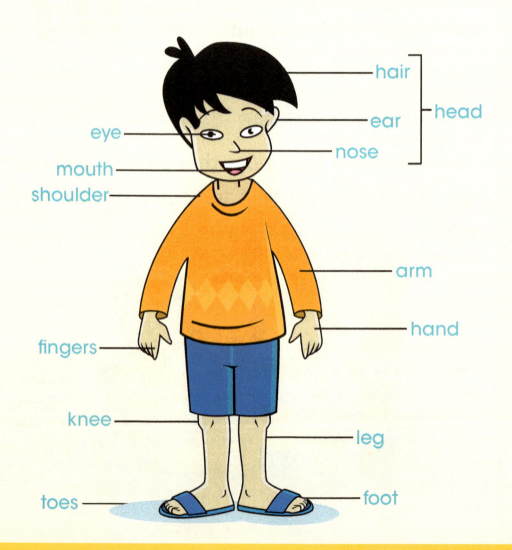

62 Glossary and index

calf	the young of a cow or elephant	10
compare	look at how things are similar and how they are different	9
concrete	a mixture of water, sand and cement that goes hard like a rock	35
different	something that is not the same	26
environment	the place in which living things live	8
fabric	a soft, flexible material used to make clothes and other things	34
farm	a place where animals or crops are produced for food	8
fast/er/est	taking a short time to get to another place	49
fat	oily or greasy material	13
feel	use the sense of touch to find out about something	31
fibres	small thread-like parts	37
flexible	when something can bend easily	36
food	what animals eat	12
glass	a material that you can see through	35
group	to put things with each other	38
grow	get bigger	18
healthy	a living thing that has all it needs and is not sick or damaged	12

Glossary and index   63

hear	you hear sounds using your ears	30
human	men, women and children are humans	11
jump	move so that you are not touching the ground	43
light	something that comes from the Sun	20
listen	you use your ears to listen to sounds	53
living	living things grow, need food, make waste, use air and have young	6
look (at)	use your eyes to find out about something	7
loud	a description of a sound	55
magnifying glass	shaped glass that makes objects look bigger	37
materials	we use materials like glass, wood, plastic and fabric to make many things that we use everyday	34
metal	a material that is often strong and shiny	34
move/ing/ment	change position	42
name	say what something is called	17
non-living	not alive	6
paper	a material that you use to write on	35
pet	an animal that you keep in the home	8
plant	a living thing that can make its own food	6
plastic	a type of material that may be coloured	34

pull	try to move something towards you	44
push	try to move something away from you	44

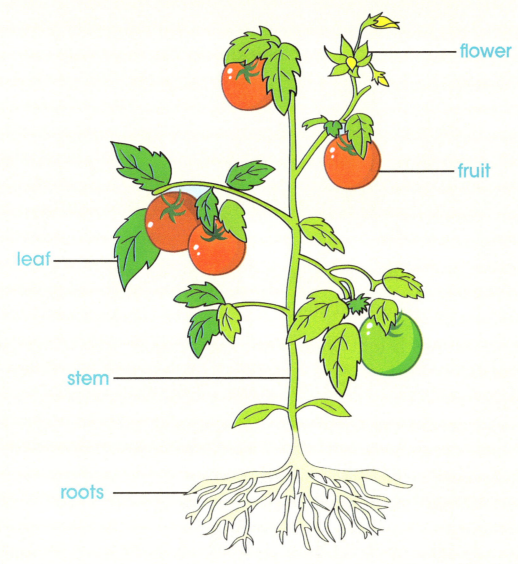

properties	the words we use to describe a material	36
question	you ask a question to find something out	21
quiet	a sound that only makes a little noise	55
recycle	when a material is used again	38
rock	hard part of the Earth	34

Glossary and index   65

rough	bumpy, not flat	37
rubber	a material that can bend easily and keeps water out	34
run	to move your feet quickly, faster than walking	43
salt	a white powder that we add to food to change the taste	13
see	to look at things with our eyes	30
seed	the part of a plant from which a new plant can grow	18
senses	the things animals use to find out about the world around them	30
shiny	looks bright when light shines on it	39
sight	you use your eyes to see things	31
similar	being the same in some ways	24
slow/er/est	taking a long time to get to another place	49
smell	you use your nose to smell things	30
smooth	flat, not bumpy	37
soft (material)	gentle to touch, not hard	36
soft (sound)	a quiet sound	55
sort	put things into groups	39
sound	something you hear	52

Glossary and index

source	where something comes from or where it is made	52
stop	not moving anymore	49
strong	powerful, not easily broken	36
sugar	a sweet white powder that we add to food and drinks	13
swing	to move backwards and forwards, as on a swing	43
taste	you taste your food using your tongue	30
test	do something to see what happens	39
tongue	the part of your mouth that helps to feel and taste food	31
touch	a sense you use to feel things	30
turn	change direction	43
voice	what you use to talk	52
water	a liquid that you drink (the sea and rivers are made of water)	19
wood	a material that comes from the trunk of a tree	34
young	a baby plant or animal that has only been alive a short time	11

Acknowledgements

The authors and publisher are grateful for the permissions granted to reproduce copyright materials. While every effort has been made, it has not always been possible to identify the sources of all the materials used, or to trace all the copyright holders. If any omissions are brought to our notice, we will be happy to include the appropriate acknowledgements on reprinting.

The publisher is grateful to the experienced teachers Mansoora Shoaib Shah, Lahore Grammar School, 55 Main, Gulberg, Lahore and Lynne Ransford for their careful reviewing of the content.

p. 7*l* Cederlund Tholin/ Shutterstock; p. 7*c* AptTone/ Shutterstock; p. 7*r* Tupungato/ Shutterstock; p. 11*l* Steve Bloom Images/ Alamy; p. 11*c* Kuttig - Animals/ Alamy; p. 11*r* Mark Bridger/ Shutterstock; p. 13 Adisa/ Shutterstock; p. 17 StudioSmart/ Shutterstock; p. 18 Scott Sinklier/AgStock Images, Inc./ Alamy; p. 19 Flavio Vallenari/ iStockphoto; p. 21 inga spence/ Alamy; p. 23*l* Nigel Cattlin/ Alamy; p. 23*r* Nigel Cattlin/ Alamy; p. 27*l* Asiaselects/ Alamy; p. 27*cl* Ocean/ Corbis; p. 27*cr* Levranii/ Shutterstock; p. 27*r* Ilike/ Shutterstock; p. 31*l* Pakhnyushcha/ Shutterstock; p. 31*cl* Catcher of Light, Inc./ Shutterstock; p. 31*cr* AfriPics.com/ Alamy; p. 31*r* paolo gislimberti/ Alamy; p. 35 Thomas Imo/ Alamy; p. 37*tr*/ Shutterstock; p. 43 Marvin Dembinsky Photo Associates/ Alamy; p. 46 Brian Davidson, U.S. Air Force/public domain/ Wikimedia Commons; p. 47 kavram/ Shutterstock; p. 51*bl* JeremyRichards/ Shutterstock; p. 51*c* Tibor Bognar/ Alamy; p. 51*tr* dominic dibbs/ Alamy; p. 51*br* irabel8/ Shutterstock; p. 54*l* Corbis/ SuperStock; p. 54*r* ollyy/ Shutterstock; p. 57 Joel Rogers/ Documentary Value/ Corbis

Cover artwork: Bill Bolton

l = left, *r* = right, *t* = top, *b* = bottom, *c* = centre